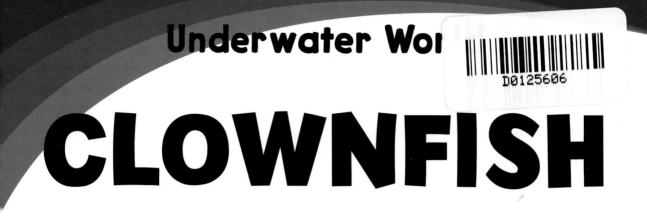

D0125606

CLOWNFISH

By Ryan Nagelhout

Gareth Stevens
Publishing

Please visit our website, www.garethstevens.com. For a free color catalog of all our high-quality books, call toll free 1-800-542-2595 or fax 1-877-542-2596.

Library of Congress Cataloging-in-Publication Data

Nagelhout, Ryan.
 Clownfish / Ryan Nagelhout.
    p. cm. — (Underwater world)
 ISBN 978-1-4339-8564-5 (pbk.)
 ISBN 978-1-4339-8565-2 (6-pack)
 ISBN 978-1-4339-8563-8 (library binding)
 1. Anemonefishes—Juvenile literature. I. Title.
 QL638.P77N34 2013
 597'.72—dc23
                                                    2012019199

First Edition

Published in 2013 by
Gareth Stevens Publishing
111 East 14th Street, Suite 349
New York, NY 10003

Copyright © 2013 Gareth Stevens Publishing

Editor: Ryan Nagelhout
Designer: Katelyn Londino

Photo credits: Cover, pp. 1, 5, 7, 9 iStockphoto/Thinkstock.com; pp. 11, 13, 24 (sea) Rich Carey/Shutterstock.com; p. 15 © iStockphoto.com/parfyonov; pp. 17, 24 (reef) © iStockphoto.com/EXTREME-PHOTOGRAPHER; p. 19 Jeff Hunter/Photographer's Choice/Getty Images; pp. 21, 24 (anemone) Frank Wasserfuehrer/Shutterstock.com; p. 23 Willyam Bradberry/Shutterstock.com.

Printed in the United States of America

CPSIA compliance information: Batch #CW13GS: For further information contact Gareth Stevens, New York, New York at 1-800-542-2595.

Contents

A clownfish has
three stripes.
It is often orange.

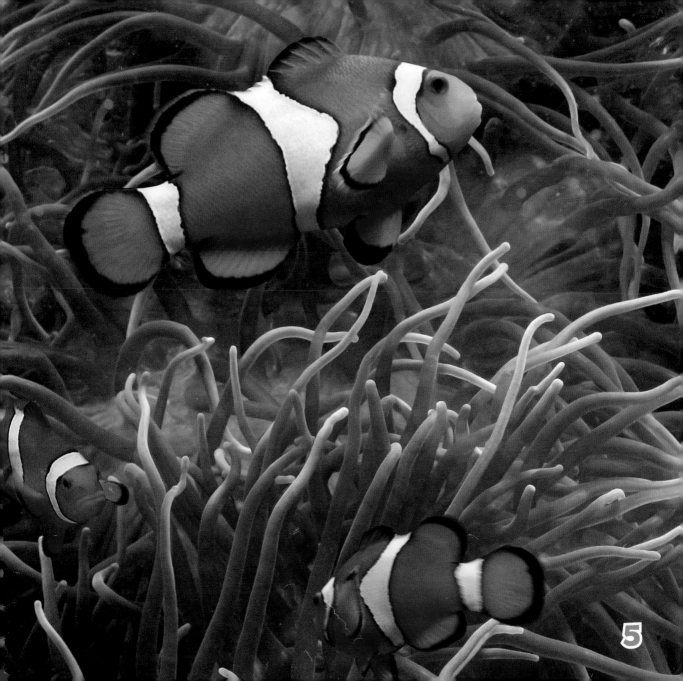

It can live
up to 10 years.

There are over
27 kinds.

It lives in the sea.

It likes to live
in warm water.

13

It swims at the sea floor.

It swims around a reef.
This is its home.

Its bright colors can bring danger.

It stays near helpful animals to live. These are called anemones.

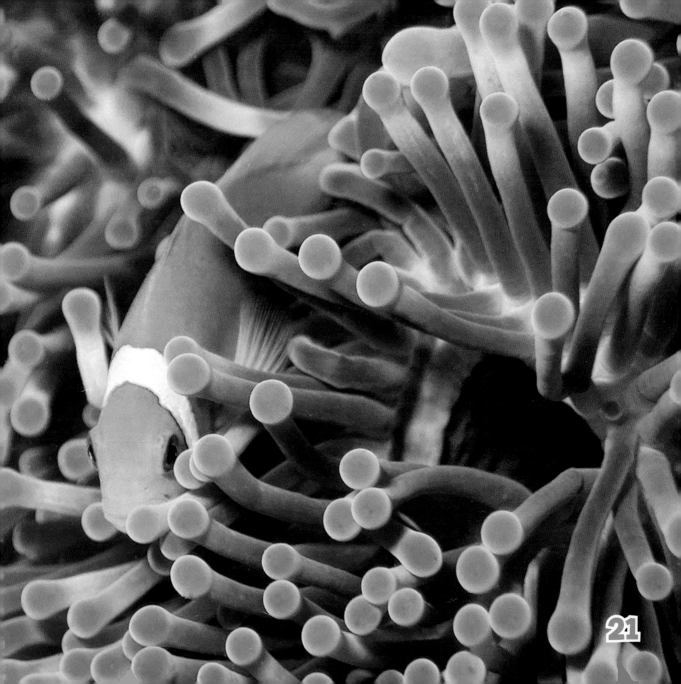

They work with each other to get food.

Words to Know

  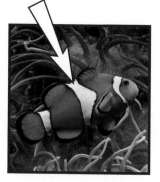

anemone   reef   stripe

Index